Affiliate Marketing

Fastest Way to Make Money Online.
Learn How to do Internet Marketing,
Easy Step by Step

Justin Gibbs
1st May, 2016

Table of Contents

Introduction 1

Benefits 2

What is Affiliate Marketing? 3

How Affiliate Marketing Works? 5

Beginners Guide to Affiliate Marketing 7

5 Blogging Tips for Affiliate Marketers 8

How to Make Money from Website via Affiliate Marketing 9

How to Start an Affiliate Program? (51 Point Checklist) 20

18 Affiliate Marketing Tips to Promote Affiliate Products 25

7 Step Affiliate Marketing Guide for Newbies 28

Affiliate Marketing 6 Key Step Success Cycle 31

Different Way to do Affiliate Marketing 33

Best Places to Find Various Affiliate Products 35

Points to Remember to Become a Successful Affiliate
.... 36

The Benefits of Affiliate Marketing 37

10 Commandments of Affiliate Marketing 41

10 Keys to Becoming an Affiliate Marketing SUPERHERO 43

How to Stand Out from All the Other Affiliates with your EMAIL MARKETING 45

The Power of Affiliate 54

Amazon Affiliate Quick Guide 56

Rakuten Affiliate Network 58

Types of Affiliate Marketing 61

The Growth of Affiliate Marketing 63

Prosperent Affiliate Marketing with Example 67

ThemeForest Affiliate Marketing with Example 71

Five Steps to Internet Marketing Success 74

16 Tips for Success in Internet Marketing 78

Marketing Tips for Affiliate Products/Services 82

Tools you Need for Affiliate Marketing 84

Conclusion 85

Legal Notice 86

Introduction

Affiliate Marketing is an intensive *eBook* for *Beginners*, to become a high-earning affiliate champion.

An affiliate business is one of the easiest ways to get your feet wet in ecommerce. You 00send visitors (i.e., potential customers) to a merchant's Web site that you are representing. If they buy or complete a required action (for example, fill in a form), the merchant pays you a commission. Simple, Right?

That, in essence, is the beauty of the affiliate concept. You can be up and building a business in record time, at minimal risk. Top-notch merchants supply everything (i.e., excellent products, ordering, credit card processing, and delivery). All you need to do is to put yourself in the path between customers and quality merchants and earn a commission for your efforts.

Benefits

Exposure is key to any component of a marketing strategy. By having affiliates, you can have your product or service held out for the online world to see. And by staying present on appropriate sites, your exposure will increase exponentially by staying in tune with the correct, targeted demographics.

Exposure also allows you to build an image and brand name. Building those allows you to leave a lasting impression on prospective customers so that they are more likely to come back and make a purchase. And because it leaves a lasting impression, that means it is likely to be spread to others through the Internet and even word of mouth.

Is affiliate marketing right for your business? This EBook will solve all your problems. For more information Contact Justin Gibbs Affiliate Marketing Expert.

What is Affiliate Marketing?

Affiliate marketing has become one of the most popular ways to make money online. It is a type of performance-based marketing in which a business/merchant rewards one or more affiliates for each visitor or customer brought by the affiliate's own marketing efforts.

Affiliate Marketing is the promotion of a product or service through a website, where in the end, the publisher(aka, owner of the website) is paid.

Affiliate marketing is a way to earn money by promoting and selling other people's products. It's the best way to earn money as there are many people who have made tons of money from it.

- The publisher helps the company promote their product via a link or code specific to the publisher.
- By clicking the link, the user is brought to another site where the good or service is being offered.
- Conversion rates of that single link or code are tracked back to the publisher.
- The publisher is paid out a percentage of the sale from the clicked link or used code.

What is an Affiliate?

An affiliate is anyone who sells, promotes or advertises a product that isn't their and gets a commission for the sale or lead generated.

An affiliate, in simple words, is a salesman who sells different products and thus earns commission through it.

How Affiliate Marketing Works?

There are 4 Kinds of People Involved

MEET STEVE: "I Run a Shoe E-Store" ADVERTISER(MERCHANT)

Generally seek to maximize sales and leads by allowing publishers to promote their products and services via affiliate campaigns.

MEET LAURA: "I Have a Blog About Shoes" PUBLISHER(AFFILIATES)

Generally seek to monetize their website traffic by promoting merchants affiliate campaigns.

MEET ANDY: "I Want to Buy Some Shoes" USER(CONSUMER)

A potential customer that is browsing the publisher's website.

MEET JACK: "We Can Help" AFFILIATE NETWORK

Provide a platform and service for Advertisers and Publisher to connect.

The Beneficial Relationship Between the Four Entities Involved

1. **LAURA** joins **STEVE's** affiliate program
2. **LAURA** place banners on her shoe blog advertising **STEVE's** shoe store
3. **ANDY** is browsing the web trying to find a cool pair of new shoes and comes across **LAURA's** blog
4. **ANDY** sees the banner and clicks on it and is directed through to **STEVE's** shoe store via an affiliate link
5. The affiliate link drops a cookie on **ANDY's** browser
6. **ANDY** buys a pair of shoes from **STEVE's** online shoe store
7. Upon purchase a tracking pixel on **STEVE's** side is matched up to the affiliate cookie on **ANDY's** browser
8. The tracking pixel and cookies shows that **LAURA** send **ANDY** to **STEVE's** site and logs a sales commission on the affiliate network
9. The Affiliate Network provides reports to both **LAURA** and **STEVE** showing all the clicks and sales that have produced through the affiliate links
10. At the end of each month the affiliate network collects the commissions from **STEVE** and makes payment to **LAURA**

Beginners Guide to Affiliate Marketing

How do i Increase my Website's Income?

Publisher or *Webmaster*

Most websites can make additional revenue by becoming an affiliate of another company.

But how does it work?

1. Publisher or webmaster chooses affiliate program and signs up
2. Publisher or webmaster integrates affiliate link onto their website
3. Publisher or webmaster promotes the merchant with unique content, reviews, and more
4. Visitors to the publisher's site visit the merchant using the affiliate link
5. Visitors that become customers earn publisher commission

Publisher is paid for any sales or referrals he makes

5 Blogging Tips for Affiliate Marketers

Build a Link With the Audience: The key factors like regularity, top quality content and user engagement are stipulation for making healthy relation and interaction with your viewers.

Focus On Your Niche: If you are trying to promote a jewellery, brand and half of the audience is not interested about it but in gadgets, you have already lost your conversion ratio by 50 percent. Therefore, niche blogging is better than general blogging!

Learn From Others: Affiliate marketing is just like an art. You have to be expert in the art of effective to be able to promote and make the sale. This art might not be natural aspect of your character, but can be learnt through others.

Choose the Right Product: Finding the right product in the right niche is very important for affiliate marketing. You have to select smartly to obtain highest possible advantages from affiliate marketing.

Try It Out: Always test product or services before being promoted, because how will you convince others, if you are not satisfied.

How to Make Money from Website via Affiliate Marketing

Beyond the basics of building a website, building an audience, and promoting a single affiliate program, take a closer look at how you can not only earn your first dollar with affiliate marketing, but how you could build your own Internet empire.

Build Brandable Websites

It's not all about the keywords. If you can include them, great.

Brandable Domains
1. Generate marketing buzz
2. Help with word-to-mouth marketing
3. Are the third most trusted advertising source

Are built around words with mass appeal.

Use tools to help you generate ideas
1. Domain Bot
2. Domain Hacks

Create Unique Content

Unique Content

- Helps search engines see your "QUALITY" when they make algorithm changes
- Gives you a chance to clearly identify and develop your brand
- Gives readers a reason to come back for more

Ask Yourself

Could this content have been created by anyone else? **=>** If the answer is yes, the content is not "UNIQUE".

Ways your Content can be UNIQUE:

Expertise: Yours is already unique. Leverage it.

Relationships: Leverage relationships with others in your niche to create powerful content to benefit both of you.

Exclusive Offers: Do something that makes your company stand out. You're not selling "a" product, you're selling "your" product.

- Look at what other affiliates are doing, and come up with a way to make your offer better.
- If it's allowed by the terms of your affiliate program:
    - Include an extra bonus
    - Offer a discount

User Generated Content Creates Dialogue

Create an avenue for your users to talk back to you.

- Allow readers to leave comments on your blog posts
- Make it easy for readers to leave product reviews/testimonials
  - *Ask permission to share them in your marketing efforts*
- Actively ask for content
  - *Blog post comments*
  - *Social media shares*
  - *Ask questions to spark Debate*

Chipotle Mexican Grill's "Wrap What You Love" Contest

- Contestants were asked to wrap their favorite things in gold or silver foil to mimic the company's business burritos and photograph the result
- Contestants uploaded the photos to the company website or Facebook page
- Winner received $10,000 for his photo of his four-day-old baby wrapped in gold foil

Honda's "Super Civic Quest" Contest

- Contestants received Facebook credits and Amazon MP3 downloads for solving clues to find a missing Mexican wrestler in a red Civic Coupe
- Contestants got to see five new Civic models and the chance to win two new Civics, one for themselves, and one for a friend.

Kraft Foods "Real Women of Philadelphia" Contest

- Asked women all over the country to create cooking videos and submit them to.
- The winner received a $25,000 talent contract, the chance to star in their own series of cooking videos, and contribution to cookbook featuring community favorite cream cheese recipes.

Make Yourself Stand Out from the Crowd

Create a point of difference (POD) so you don't blend in with all the other affiliates promoting the same products and services you are.

Figure out how your product is different in terms of
- Price
- Benefits
- Convenience
- Features
- Availability
- Customer Service

Craft your story
- Why are you in business?
- How do you do business?
- Where do you do business?

Market your POD everywhere!
- Business Cards
- Your Website
- Company Name and Tagline
- Logo
- Email Signature
- Social Media Profiles

Use Multiple Methods to Diversify Your Monetization

Multiple affiliate programs

Create a broad source of information on a topic and use it to leverage multiple PM programs.

For Example:

NotWithoutSalt.com is a comprehensive source of information on cooking and recipes, and uses affiliate programs for:

- *Cooking Utensils*
- *Ingredients*

Sell advertising

Create a page dedicated to advertising space options.

Note your traffic volume and other reasons why people should advertise with you.

Give regular discounts to entice advertisers.

Keep it easy to maintain on your end with a WordPress plugin such as OIO Publisher or WP 125.

Pitch advertisers directly

Note your traffic volume and other reasons why people should advertise with you.

Give regular discounts to entice advertisers.

- *Find advertisers by using Adsense on your website for a few days.*
- *Watch the ads that are displayed and where they come from*
- *Contact those companies directly with an attractive offer*

Reach out to merchants to become affiliates for them

Know of a product or service you'd love to promote, but don't see an affiliate program for them?

- *Talk to the merchant directly.*
- *Offer information about your background and why you would make the perfect affiliate.*
- *Negotiate a deal.*

Develop Methods to Contact Users without them Having to Visit Your Website

Email is personal and direct

It's a powerful marketing tool because:

- It's permission-based.
- No social media algorithms to trick.
- No sponsored tweets to "beat".
- No Pinterest worthy graphics are necessary.

Connect and build relationships with your customers.

You're not competing for attention in a busy social media atmosphere.

You've got their personal, private attention their email box.

Produce Blog Content and Get RSS Subscribers

Quality blog content keeps your website fresh and up to date.

Blogs can produce user generated content.

Promote your RSS feed: It's another way to get into people's email boxes.

- Promote your feed:
  - Off your blog
  - Email signatures
- Social media
- At key entry points on your blog.
- Offer a bonus to subscribers, such a as a free ebook.

Create a Facebook fan page.
Build your Audience
- Invite your friends.
- Share your page.
- Invite business contacts.

Create Content
- Think about what your customers want.
  - Photos
  - Links

Be Authentic
- Share what you're excited about. Your customers will be excited, too.

Be Responsive
- When someone comments on a post, respond to them.
  - If they're asking a question and you need more time, let them know they're on your radar.

Be Consistent
- Post regularly.
  - The more you post, the more you have to engage fans with.
- Create a schedule to maximize your time.

Replicate Success
- Use the Page Insights tool to see what your audience is responding to.
- When you find something they respond to, do it again.

Create a Twitter Account

Build your Audience
- Listen to what others are saying
- Share your account with current customers, friends, and business contacts

Attract Followers
- Give incentive to follow you on Twitter
  - Example: Get a 10% off coupon for your next order just for following us on Twitter!

Integrate Twitter with your other efforts
- Add a link to your Twitter profile on your website. Let your followers on other platforms know about your Twitter account

Be Authentic
- Follow the same principle as with Facebook here

Be Responsive
- Look for people talking about your business
  - Talk to them
- If someone tweets you, respond as soon as possible

Be Consistent
- Tweet on a regular basis
  - The more you post, the more you'll have to engage followers with
  - Use a schedule to help maximize your time

Develop Relationships with Others in Your Niche
- Research. Who are the most powerful people in your niche?
- Follow the powerful people you want to develop relationships with.
- Interact with them on their websites and various social media channels
  - Link to their content
  - Share their social media posts with your audience
  - Retweet their tweets
- Monitor and track your relationships
  - What good, if any, is coming of them?
  - Think about what you have to offer each other, and how you can create something of mutual benefit

How to Start an Affiliate Program? (51 Point Checklist)

1. Who are your customers?
2. Who are your competitors?
3. Research affiliate programs run by your competitors
   a. Public or private program?
   b. Which software/network used?
   c. How do affiliates join?
   d. Commission type and amount?
   e. How much revenue do affiliate drive?
4. Setup your goals?
   a. Who are your affiliates?
   b. How many affiliates do you want?
   c. How much revenue are you expecting per affiliate?
   d. Target a percentage of revenue through affiliate
5. Do your calculations (use Excel)
   a. Total affiliates expected
   b. Commissions paid out
   c. Total affiliate revenue
   d. Total profit
   e. Expenses
   f. Net Profit

6. Setup a budget
   a. Amount spend for attracting new affiliates
   b. Amount/Percentage spend for affiliate payouts
   c. Amount spend for prizes, bonuses, incentives
7. Choose your affiliate management platform
   a. Affiliate network
   b. In house affiliate management
   c. Outsourced program management
8. Choose your commission model
   a. PPC (Pay Per Click)
   b. PPS (Pay Per Sale)
   c. PPL (Pay Per Lead)
9. Fix the payment terms
   a. Minimum amount for payout
   b. Payment cycle NET15, NET30, NET60
   c. Payment methods
10. Finalize the commission amount
    a. Fixed amount
    b. Percentage of sale
11. Create a search marketing policy
12. Create a trademark usage policy for affiliates

13. Create an "Affiliate Program" page on your website
14. Create a policy for fraud orders
15. Create a policy for refunded orders
16. Create an "Affiliate Agreement" merging all these policies
17. Create promo banners and logos that affiliates can use
18. Create reprint articles, brandable reports and emails promos
19. Invite your own customers to join your affiliate program
20. Introduce the affiliate program in your company's newsletter
21. Announce the affiliate program on your blog
22. Promote it to your Fans and Followers (Facebook and Twitter)
23. Reach out to affiliates directly via affiliate forums
24. Submit your affiliate program to different affiliate directories
25. Seek joint venture partners and contact them individually
26. Use affiliate recruitment agencies
27. Approve affiliate applications manually to filter the genuine ones

28. Send a welcome email to all your affiliates

29. Provide them direct contact details of their affiliate manager

30. Send weekly/monthly newsletter to your affiliate base announcing new promotions and suggesting ways to promote your product

31. Run incentive based contests for affiliates

32. Provide them tools and tips to increase conversion rate

33. Communicate with affiliates personally

34. Provide promotional material
    a. Articles
    b. Banners and Logos
    c. Emails

35. Special treatment for high performing affiliates
    a. Special coupons
    b. Promotional emails
    c. Brochures

36. Keep a close watch on daily clicks, conversions and EPC

37. Match conversions in your affiliate program with your CRM

38. Reject conversions that are marked as fraud in your CRM

39. Keep a close watch on traffic: countries, referring URL's promotional methods
40. Check exact payments (Keep in mind refunds, fraud transactions)
41. Pay affiliates on time based on payment cycle
42. Incentives, bonuses can be paid out based on payment cycle
43. Track all sales by affiliates
44. Track conversion rates of all affiliates
45. Learn from their sales process and improve and marketing channels
46. Prepare a list of blacklisted affiliates
47. Evaluate current affiliate promo materials
48. Replace expired materials if required
49. On-going market analysis of competitors
50. Drive new affiliates consistently
51. Keep your affiliates happy
    a. Prizes
    b. Contests
    c. Increased Payouts

18 Affiliate Marketing Tips to Promote Affiliate Products

1. **Seasonal Content and Promotions:** Keep up with holidays and what's happening year-round. Offer timely content and promotions on a regular basis

2. **Coupons:** Coupon codes are a great way to draw in new customers. Get promo codes from the product owner

3. **Free Samples and Trials:** Let potential buyers experience and taste the product before buying. Free samples and trials tend to always be winners

4. **Live Teleseminars/Webinars:** Schedule content-rich events that promote your affiliate products

5. **Audio Recordings:** Whether it's an interview or just content-rich recordings, create audios and give them away free

6. **Videos:** Create a variety of types of videos from interviews, to instructional, screen capture videos and product walkthroughs.

7. **Interviews**: Interview the product owner/creator. Get the owner of the product to provide useful content and answers to the common questions about the product

8. **Product Reviews**: Create product reviews with product specifications, quotes from customers and more

9. **Special Reports**: Take content a bit further and create short special reports that you give away free. Brand your document with your affiliate link

10. **Blog Posts**: Along the same lines as an article, a blog post can be a bit more personal and friendly in nature

11. **Articles**: Targeted articles that include your product as part of the solutions to a problem can be very effective for sales

12. **Twitter Tweets**: Everyone's tweeting these days. Give a little blurb promotion(up to 140 characters, with spaces). Remember, to leave room for you affiliate link too.

a. **Hint**: Use the headline from the sales letter

13. **Long Text/Email Solo Ads**: Direct response emails create some of the best sales and opt in conversion rates. So send emails to your list and consider doing solo emails via Safe-Swaps.com

14. **Pay-Per-Click Ads**: Leverage Google AdWords, Facebook Ads and Facebook Mobile Ads as well as other Mobile Ad Networks like AdMob

15. **Short Text Ads:** Provide short text blurbs in email and blog content

16. **Banners and Graphics**: Use a variety of sizes for your best converting affiliate offers. Also, help your readers by updating the graphics seasonally or for specific promotions automatically

17. **Landing Pages for Different Audiences**: Target your affiliate landing pages as much as possible

18. **Inline Text Links to Products and Specific Pages**: Make it easier for your readers of html emails and blogs click directly to your affiliate offers

7 Step Affiliate Marketing Guide
for Newbies

1. **<u>WEBSITE</u>:** A website is a great place to start affiliate marketing. The quickest and easiest way to set up a website is WordPress. A self hosted WordPress installation is the perfect start for an affiliate marketer.

2. **<u>CHOOSING A TOPIC (NICHE)</u>:** Choosing a topic for your website is Azan important step. When starting out, it is suggested you choose ONE topic that you are interested or passionate about. This way it will be easier to add content to your website.

3. **<u>CONTENT</u>:** You will want to add content to your website on a regular basis. Using a web platform like WordPress makes that easier. The content should be high quality and original. Ensure that Your content is interesting or helpful. High quality, consistently added content is the key to a successful website.

4. **FIND OFFERS**: Find offers that match your content. There are many different offers online so you can monetize just about any passion. Most major online retailers have affiliate programs. Some of the most popular are:

a. Amazon - https://affiliate-program.amazon.com/

b. Ebay - http://www.ebaypartnernetwork.com

c. ClickBank - http://www.clickbank.com

d. Commission Junction - http://www.cj.com/

e. Shore A Sale - http://www.shareasale.com/

f. Linkshare - http://www.linkshare.com/

g. Google- http://www.google.com/ads/affiliatenetwork/

5. **ADD YOUR ADS/LINKS**: These sites will give you affiliate links or html ad code to put on your site. Add the links/ads to your website. If you used WordPress you can add the ads to your sidebar and/or individual posts.

6. **YOUR TRAFFIC ACTS**: When someone on your website clicks an ad or link and then buys - you earn a commission! Some affiliate offers don't even require a purchase, just an action to be taken like your referral signing up for a free trial.

7. **<u>YOU GET PAID!</u>**: You will get paid by whatever affiliate companies you use to monetize your website. Make sure you check the terms of each network. There are different payout thresholds, methods and requirements on each site. Each site will also have it's own report system so you can check out how many people are clicking your link/ads, how much you have earned and how many people have seen your ads/links.

<u>REPEAT WHAT WORKS</u>: When you have a successful affiliate website you knows what goes into making one. Now you can create other affiliate sites based on different niches. Just took what worked from your first site and apply it to your second. This will help you grow your revenues exponentially!

Affiliate Marketing 6 Key Step Success Cycle

1. **Pick a Niche**: Choose a market instead of a product. The reason for this is so that you can put more products in your pipeline. Choose a market which you are interested in and obtain detailed information about it.

2. **Find Affiliate Offers**: Once you've chosen your market, it's time to select the products you would like to promote through affiliate networks such as ShareaSale, CommissionJunction, Clickbank, etc. Find out about the offers such as commissions, conversion rates and promotional materials provided by the merchant.

3. **Build an E-Mail Autoresponder**: Create an e-mail autoresponder series which includes information about your product. You can build a series of some basic information or provide tips about the niche you are in. Be creative and always remember to focus on adding value to your subscribers. Remember to add your affiliate link in your e-mails when you send them to your merchant's offer page

4. **<u>Build a Lead Capture Page</u>**: If you are building a business, having a website is necessary. This website will be needed to show your affiliate products and grab the visitor's email. Create a page in your website where you will capture information about your prospect so you can send them to your email autoresponder series.

5. **<u>Generate Traffic</u>:** Once your website is up, generate traffic using techniques such as SEO, Pay-Per-Click, Social Media, Video Marketing, etc. Try different techniques and see what gets you the best results. Continue with the technique that shows best results from the basics of your experience.

6. **<u>Get Paid and Repeat</u>**: Once you have started to make a good and reliable income with a single product, you should add more products to your autoresponder pipeline. Rinse and repeat the process to scale up your affiliate campaigns and income.

Different Way to do Affiliate Marketing

1. **Writing Blog Posts**: If you have a blog then you can use your blog to promote the affiliate products. Write a genuine review of the product and compel your readers to buy it. Having a blog is the best thing, you easily promote products and enjoy the huge affiliate commissions.

2. **E-Mail Marketing**: It is the best way known to get more and more sales. If you have a large or a decent number of subscribers then you can generate tons of money out of it. Just build your email subscribers list and create campaigns to promote different products.

3. **Web 2.0 Properties**: To reach a wider audience, you need to use Web 2.0 properties to promote the products. Use Web 2.0 sites like HubPages and StumbleUpon to gain more exposure and thus an increased sales.

4. **Article Directories**: You can even use Article Directories to maximise your affiliate earnings. There are Dozens of article Directories like Ezinearticles, GoArticles etc., you can use to promote your products. But such Directories with caution, as some directories don't allow to add affiliate links in articles.

5. **Other Ways**: Don't just limit yourself to the above ways of promoting affiliate proDucts. Use your own imagination and find out new way to promote products and earn large sum of affiliate commission.

Best Places to Find Various Affiliate Products

ClickBank: The best and the most popular place to find a wide range of products. ClickBank is very user-friendly and you will easily be able to find the best products.

Commission Junction: Commission Junction is the biggest and the best marketplace for affiliates. You will find different products with the help of the wee-organised directory.

ShareaSale: ShareaSale runs a network of great number of affiliates with hundreds of merchant programs to promote. You can easily find products and increase your affiliate income.

LinkShare: LinkShare is the best place to find a large range of e-commerce companies willing to advertise. Also find some of the best affiliate programs with high commissions.

Points to Remember to Become a Successful Affiliate

1. Select the merchants very carefully and research about their background before going ahead.
2. Choose the products that comes under your niche, if you own a blog or a website.
3. If you have a blog, then add banners containing affiliate links in it.
4. Before writing a review of any product with an intention to promote it, its the best if you use the product before and write a genuine review of the product. You can even offer an e-book on some useful points of the product or any other such stuff. Like this, you can expect a high sales.
5. Try to build it subscribers list and carry out email campaigns to promote the products. This is one of the best and most used methods.
6. Lastly, it's you who is an affiliate, think of some extra-ordinary ways to promote products and increase sales and thus your affiliate commission.

The Benefits of Affiliate Marketing

Affiliate Marketing - Paying a commission for a set of affiliates to independently advertise your brand - is sometimes overlooked in the slew of online marketing opportunities. But for those in the know, affiliate marketing with its unique set of advantages, is an essential part of an effective online marketing strategy

1. Cost
2. Risk
3. Time and Energy
4. Diversity
5. Popularity

Cost

- **Pay-for-Performance**: With affiliate marketing you only pay if a certain predetermined action is met. This could be a click-through revenue or market information. No payment without results

- **Fixed Costs**: You also specify what action will pay what amount. You always know what the rates will be.

- **By Comparison Search Engine Optimization(SEO) Development**: Just to increase your site's pagerank can cost $76-$200 hourly per project, those costs can reach anywhere between $1,000 and $7,500

Risk

- **Low Risk**: Affiliate marketing is considered very low risk, because you don't have to pay if it doesn't work. You don't have to invest capital in a strategy that might not pan out.
- **Market Comparison**: Low-risk means that affiliate marketing is ideal for exploring new markets. While a whole new international marketing plan might be cost-prohibitive. Affiliate marketing provides low overhead while giving you access to local marketing experts

Time and Energy

- **By Comparison**: Social media marketing takes a good deal of time and energy creating new content, replying to comments and relaying content to different sites.
  - Customizable programs marketing doesn't have to be time consuming.
- **Many Merchants Use**
  - **Affiliate Network**: Select a network that will take care of everything for you, including giving creative help.
  - **Third Party Hosting**: Leave the infrastructure up to the third party but still set up your own terms and payment.

Diversity

- **<u>Many Birds, One Stone</u>:** Affiliate advertising is a great way to utilize other forms of online marketing for a lower cost. Affiliates will use their own skills to get your brand noticed
  - 80% SEO
  - 60% Social Networking
  - 60% Blogging
  - 40% Email Marketing
- **<u>And More</u>:** Developing an individual program for all of these aspects would take far more time and more importantly far more money

Popularity

- SEO lead the way in popularity and far other strategies in the amount spent on it.
- Social network marketing gets a lot of hype, and is growing in investment.
- Retailer, financial services firms and online education providers are restricted to the top three providers.
- However, affiliate marketing is gaining traction as a low-risk, high-return investment.

Not a Regular Job

- As an affiliate-marketing publisher, you can create a steady flow of income, even when you're not at your computer.

Popular

- 42.9% of affiliate-marketing publisher say they operate 2 to 5 websites to promote affiliate programs and the number of the publishers is growing.

Easy-Tracking

- Affiliate programs provide campaign statistics that measure their effectiveness.

No Need to Sell Anything

- Just create good content and recommend products based on your experience

10 Commandments of Affiliate Marketing

1. **Know Your Audience**: Catering to your audience is crucial. Determine why visitors are coming to your site and tailor it to fit their needs.

2. **Be Trustworthy**: Customers can detect a site that sells a useless product. Run affiliate sites with the aim of earning repeat business through usefulness.

3. **Be Helpful**: Create a useful resource. Promote products you believe in and include good descriptions, or reviews, of the products to give customers a reason to use your site

4. **Be Transparent**: Customers can detect a cover-up. Disclose all your affiliations so customers don't bypass your site out of spite.

5. **Design Carefully**: Finding the right site design is important. Try different products, ads, graphics, and text to find the most effective formula.

6. **Try Different Programs**: Each affiliate program is different. Sift through the wide variety of programs and the features they offer to find which is most effective for your site.

7. **Make Content Timeless**: Customers disregard dated information. Include links to your updated information on any outdated pages.

8. **Be Patient**: Lifetime payout programs can take some time to grow. Continue to maintain old referral links while creating new ones.

9. **Stay Relevant**: Programs are constantly updating their offerings. Don't be left in the dust by using dated ads while your competitors feature superior content

10. **Content Matters**: Customers come to your site for its content. Don't solicit your site to the whims of a questionable easy money affiliate program.

10 Keys to Becoming an Affiliate Marketing SUPERHERO

1. **Research Product Demand**: Find out whether the product you want to promote is in high demand. If it is, your chances of generating sales are greater.

2. **Choose the Right Merchant**: Protect your online reputation by choosing affiliate-marketing advertisers with a good reputation. Companies with good customer service usually have satisfied customers. So check before recommending the merchant to your readers.

3. **Choose Only Good Products**: Based on your experience, choose good products that are relevant to topics you write about.

4. **Put your Audience First**: Protect your audience. Give them only relevant content. It is better to recommend the product than to tell your readers to buy the product.

5. **Create Good Content**: Solid copywriting and content marketing are essential to your success in affiliate marketing. Learn more about creating a good content with GetResponse training materials.

6. **Engage your Readers**: There's nothing worse than a boring website. Keep your reader's attention with clear calls to action, relevant content, and attractive graphics.

7. **Build Solid Relationships**: Make a good first impression. Don't take your subscribers for granted. Show them how much you appreciate them.

8. **Use Several Traffic Sources**: Most affiliate marketing publishers promote products only on their websites. You may get better results with more sources. Run tests with pay-per-click, display advertising, guest blogging, social media and word-of-mouth advertising.

9. **Test, Measure and Track**: Most affiliate programs enable you to measure the results 1 of your campaigns. GetResponse gives you real-time tracking and statistics.

10. **Stay Current with New Trends**: Affiliate marketers test new methods to get more leads. Use GetResponse top-notch marketing materials to stay on top of the latest trends.

How to Stand Out from All the Other Affiliates with your EMAIL MARKETING

Affiliate marketing offers many attractive benefits because you can promote another company's product and receive a commission for sales without having to debelop the product, provide customers support, or hire employees to do those things for you.

However, because affiliate marketing offers these benefits you may find that it is hard to stand out among all the competition

Here are 7 Ways to use EMAIL MARKETING to Crush your Competition and bring in consistent revenue from affiliate marketing.

1. **Write your Own EMAILS:**
   a. Most affiliate programs provide ad copy and email swipe files for use in promoting their products.
   b. While you can certainly get some copy points from these materials, you don't want to fall in the trap that many affiliates do by mailing affiliate swipe to their lists.

c. There are many reasons why mailing out affiliate 'copy and paste swipe emails can hurt your conversions. The biggest reason is that your readers expect emails from you and when you mail someone else's copy and sign your name at the bottom, you're potentially saying the same thing as all the other affiliates. That's no way to stand out. Besides, your subscribers may well notice that the wording of the affiliate swipe is different from what you normally say and that can harm your conversions by annoying your subscribers. By mailing your own email copy, even if it was written by your staff copywriter, at least your email still has a shot at standing out from all the other competitors.

2. **<u>Add Value</u>:**

a. At the most basic level, an affiliate promotions says "I recommend this product, you should buy it" to your subscriber. In some cases, that may be sufficient.

b. But if all your competitors do that, you have an opportunity to stand out from the crowd by offering genuine value.

c. For example, if you are in the fitness niche, you could use the affiliate product you are promoting and share the details of your experience. Many affiliates won't take the time to do this, so if you do your promotions will stand out. Another benefit of using the product and reviewing it is that is the most valuable form of affiliate marketing. The reason the vendor is paying you a commission is for your referral, but the power of your referral will increase if your word means a lot to your subscriber. And the best way to have your recommendation carry weight is to provide your own user experience with a product as the basis of your recommendation.

d. In other words, never promote something you don't endorse. If you never use the product, you don't really know if you can endorse it, can you?

e. Authenticity is at a premium and your subscribers will likely reward an honest review better than plain old affiliate swipe copy. And the trust that follows from that authenticity can lead to higher conversions.

3. **ZIG When They ZAG:**

   a. As such, you want to point out benefits that the others do not (or overlook). For example, if you are an affiliate for the iPhone 6 and your competition is talking about its sleek looks, you could take a different approach.

   b. You could talk about how you used the built in camera and video recorder to tape a Vegas wedding on last minute notice.

   c. You could show clips of video and tell the story of how glad you were that you had bought the iPhone 6 because our friend dragged you to Vegas and all you had time to grab was your phone.

   d. Even though you're competing affiliates have the same phone to promote, your story could help you stand out and make the purchase more compelling to your subscribers.

4. **Add a Bonus**:
   a. Many successful affiliates use added bonuses to entice subscribers to buy through their affiliate link. To continue the iPhone 6 example, you might have an ebook or video of how you shot the wedding with your iPhone.
   b. Or maybe you have 10 tips and tricks for how to get the best apps or add ons for iPhones.
   c. As long as your bonus adds value, it can be used to increase sales. Two things to remember when it comes to bonuses.
   d. They must have a high perceived value to your lab target marketing AND you should consider restricting the number of bonuses by time or quantity.
   e. By having scarcity, you can motivate your buyers to choose your link and to do it quickly instead of procrastinating.

5. **<u>MAIL More Often</u>:**

   a. The lazy affiliate will just blast out one email and move on to the next offer. If you mail more frequently you have the potential to capture more sales, especially if the vendor is launching the product and a lot of affiliates are mailing at the same time.

   b. Mailing more often doesn't mean sending the same message more frequently. Instead, by mapping out a sequence of promotional emails for an affiliate offer, you could build an informative narrative and go deeper in your reasons why someone should buy the product through your affiliate link.

   c. For example, with the iPhone 6 you could do a series on the improvements over the previous version, how the iPhone 6 is better than the Samsung Galaxy competitor, and why the iPhone is easier to use, etc. If you focus your sequence of emails to address common objections to buying iPhones, you can do quite well with this approach because you are essentially laying a solid foundation for a buying decision. At the very least, you are going above and beyond what your competitors are doing with their promotions so once again, you stand out.

6. **Address Flaws**:

    a. Let's say that you happen to know there are some things about the iPhone 6 that you don't like. Maybe the phone is so slick and sleek that it's slippery and easy to drop.

    b. Or maybe the screen is so big that you find yourself watching too many YouTube videos on it instead of working. These kinds of minor flaws do several things when you point them out.

    c. First, you build credibility because you are not just a cheerleader for the product but rather an honest consumer. Second, you allow your subscribers to imagine what it is like to own the product by sharing a real user experience. This authenticity can help them make the buying decision if they relate to what you've shared.

    d. Don't worry about spooking them from buying. The reality is they had doubts of their own, at least now they know you're an honest broker. And, it's not like you're going to be citing major flaws that would be deal breakers... otherwise you shouldn't be promoting the product.

7. **<u>Add a Guarantee</u>:**
    a. Or maybe you could guarantee that if they return their purchase and the vendor doesn't provide a refund as promised, then YOU will give them a refund.
    b. Obviously, such guarantees are situation dependent and require that you have a high degree of trust in the vendor and their product.
    c. In certain circumstances where you really believe in a product and want to go all out, you could offer some kind of guarantee that goes over and above what the vendor offers. Maybe you'll give them one of your products if they don't like the one you are recommending.

In today's hectic world consumers are looking for help in deciding what to buy because they don't have time to personally evaluate everything and they want opinions they can trust.

Therefore there is a real niche for the affiliate email marketer who offers value over and above what the competition is doing.

Since the affiliate doesn't have product development, customer support, and many other burdens that a product vendor does, it pays to put in the extra effort to stand out from all the other affiliates.

After all, you've got to give your subscribers a reason to buy from you and not another affiliate because the product is the same.

Engaging with Consumers
1. Catalyst
2. Evaluation
   a. Coupon and Deal
   b. Search
   c. Content and Community
   d. Ad Network
   e. Loyalty and Rewards
   f. Software and Technology
3. Conversion
   a. Coupon Deal
   b. Loyalty and Rewards
4. Post Conversion
   a. Content and Community
5. Loyalty Loop

The Affiliate marketing channel, with its unique, high performance online publishers, has the power to influence and connect with the new consumer at critical points in their decision journey

Catalyst: A consumer decides they are in need of a product or service with a short list of brands in mind

Evaluation: The consumer adds or subtracts brands as they evaluate options and interact with online publishers

Conversion: The moment a consumer selects a particular brand and takes action at the point of conversion

Post Conversion: The consumer builds expectations based on their brand experience, influencing their next decision journey

Loyalty Loop: In today's digital world, even the most widely-recognized industry leaders must win back the well-informed consumer after every single purchase

WordPress Site Setup

8 steps to help get you started with an Amazon Affiliate Site!

Niche Selection: Find a niche that gets traffic, isn't dominated and that you can curate/create content

Hosting and Domain: Where do you think you'll get most business from given your niche? Is there an exact match domain?

Amazon Affiliate Sign Up: Create your affiliate(associate) account at http://affiliate-program.amazon.com

WordPress Theme and Plugin Selection: Find a suitable theme for affiliate sites and get the required plugins

Site Structure and Build: Be niche focused when considering your site structure and URL slugs as well as throughout the build process

Logo/Branding: Put a bit of polish on your affiliate site as it can help with conversions

Social Media Setup: Secure your social media real estate to compliment your affiliate site

Fill your Shelves: Time to find the best products from amazon for your niche and add them to your site!

#1 Affiliate Network

Rakuten LinkShare has been voted the #1 Affiliate Network for three consecutive years.

96% of Advertisers would recommend RAKUTEN LINKSHARE

81% of Publishers say RAKUTEN LINKSHARE is the best

84% of Clients see increase in revenue growth YOY

Migrating Clients: Over half experienced growth +34% YOY

On Average 84% of Clients who migrate to RAKUTEN LINKSHARE network see an increase in revenue growth year over year. Over half of those migrations see revenue growth of over 34% year over year.

Department Stores: +41% YOY After Migration

On average 2-3x higher than previous network growth rates!

Footwear: UP 34% YOY After Migration

On average 2x higher than previous network growth rates!

Apparel: UP 28% YOY After Migration

On average 2-3x higher than previous network growth rates!

United States Network Sales: Were up over 25% year over year.

In the past year, RAKUTEN LINKSHARE seen an increase in converting publishers in the following categories
1. Comparison Shopping
2. Couponmall
3. Search
4. Loyalty/Rewards
5. Deal

Quality: RAKUTEN LINKSHARE provide the perfect mix of exclusivity and variety. RAKUTEN LINKSHARE screening process is thorough to ensure our clients work with most exclusive partners. Not to mention, RAKUTEN LINKSHARE is the only network with dedicated analysts who work with you to optimize your program.

Technology: RAKUTEN LINKSHARE has a heavy investment in new technology and eCommerce expertise. US network mobile orders are up 87% year over year and we are the network leader for mobile tracking and reporting.

Types of Affiliate Marketing

Affiliate Marketing programs has never been as popular before as it is today. Why? There can be a number of reasons. The most probable reason, however, could be the fact that the benefits of affiliate marketing have become clearer to a lot of people now than they were before.

Unattached Affiliate Marketing

These are your basic pay-per-click affiliate marketing campaigns where you have no presence and no authority in the niche of the product you're promoting. There's no connection between you and the end consumer, and all you're doing is putting an affiliate link in front of someone via Google Adwords, Facebook ads, etc. in the hopes that they'll click on your link, buy the product and you'll earn a commission.

Related Affiliate Marketing

Another form of affiliate marketing is what I like to call related affiliate marketing. This is where you have some sort of presence online, whether it's through a blog, a podcast, videos, or whatever—and you have affiliate links to products related to your niche, but they're for products you don't actually use.

Involved Affiliate Marketing

Involved affiliate marketing is where you've used a product or service, truly believe in it and personally recommend it to your audience. Not in a banner ad or somewhere that says "recommended resources," but within your content, as part of your life and strategy for whatever it is you're talking about. The product almost becomes something people "have to have," because it's part of the process.

The Growth of Affiliate Marketing

Affiliate marketing is also known as "Performance-Based Marketing".

It refers to publishing links, banners and information about products/services on a website or blog and then receiving a sales commission when people click on the banners/links and then make a purchase on the advertiser's website.

United States affiliate marketing spending will be increased bt 256% in 7 years.

77% of advertisers increased their affiliate marketing spend this year, while 71% expected spend to grow in the future.

- 50% of advertisers saw a lack of respectable understanding of affiliate marketing at the level of the CEO.
- 93% of advertisers support affiliate marketing as an effective marketing channel.
- 25% of advertisers spent over one-fifth of their overall marketing spend on affiliate marketing.

Affiliate marketing is an exploding opportunity for many businesses. This is because it's cost effective and drives incremental revenue. It's a great way for businesses to diversify their traffic sources.

What Was Affiliate Marketing Like 10 Years Ago?

Amazon.com was one of the first companies to embrace affiliate marekting. Today, Amazon is still a big player, but many others have joined in, providing a huge variety of affiliate programs. These include 1000's of ecommerce websites that you can be affiliated with to earn commissions.

As we learn more about the way the Internet and trends work, we come to understand more about the way people make purchases.

As the industry grows, we are likely to see more networks and agencies bringing more affiliates to the table. Simply put, affiliate marketing has a ton of upside!

What About Future Affiliate Expansion?

As companies continue to seek exciting opportunities, the affiliate channel will no doubt be embraced more so over time.

This is because it is one of the most effective ways to gain website traffic and brand advocates.

Affiliates stand to benefit in the corning years. They will see better products, better offers, and better results.

- It's important to realize that a lot of hard work is required to be a productive affiliate.
- It'll be essential for affiliates and publishers to remain dedicated.
- If they want to stay ahead of the curve. Content production and social media are the 2 most important areas in affiliate marketing looking forward.

It's a very exciting time to be involved in the affiliate marketing industry.

- The affiliate industry is starting to mature as companies seek to regulate and control their affiliate channel.
- Growth is also being driven by improved affiliate site content and more transparency within affiliate networks.

The future of affiliate marketing looks extremely bright, as more companies embrace the channel and more affiliates get into the industry.

Mixpression

Turn ordinary images into beautiful, shoppable content. Upload your image, tag it with products, then embed it in your page and share it to social media.

ProsperLinks

With one simple script, we automatically convert any retail links on your site into links that earn you money.

Get Links

Need a quick link to a product or retailer? Our Get Links tool helps you search over 70 million products, and get links to nearly 50,000 retailers. Earn money for every sale!

Wordpress Plugin

Focus on writing great content! Our plugin helps you insert products into posts, and can even add an entire store to your blog with just a few clicks.

Developer API

Have an app and need product data? Our product API is fast, and allows for unlimited access to millions of products from top retailers.

Detailed Reporting
Let our reporting dashboard tell you what works. We tell you where every commission came from and give you tips to earn even more.

Increased Commissions
Earn higher commissions instead of negotiating commissions on your own by using Prosperent's established relationships with top merchants.

Instant Access to Merchants
Connect with Prosperent's huge network of leading merchants automatically upon sign-up. Immediately show products from any of our 39,509 merchants.

ProsperLink
This is the simplest way to make money from Prosperent as it converts your hyperlinks to the merchant sites into affiliate links. This way you will make a commission out of every successful sale. Under this, they have Link optimizer which automatically adds affiliate links into the words which have chances of making money. Specially if you have tons of non-affiliated links to Amazon site, this feature will automatically convert it into money links. Phrase link is another nifty feature which will convert word/phrase of your choice into affiliate links and help you to make more money.

ProsperAds

Prosperads are responsive ads (Works on all the devices) and it shows ads based on retargeting. That means, it shows highly targeted ads based on users earlier browsing experience. Though this is a display ads, but you will make money for sales and not for clicks. This is one reason, I suggest you to use ProsperAds on the website where you get highly targeted niche traffic. For example, fashion blog and so on.

API

This is technically for developers to pull up products from their Database and show it on your website. If implemented properly, you will end up earning a lot from your E-commerce or a review site. What really amused me about this performance based ad network is the clean and easy to use dashboard. Their dashboard is one the best I have seen in recent time, and you will find it easy to create ads, add your website and make changes. Here is a screenshot for your reference:

How to Implement Ads on your Blog

Implementing Prosperent ads on your blog is quite easy, as you can simply add few lines of Javascript on your blog and it will start converting your links into affiliate links. Do remember, using Javascript will not affect your blog SEO, whereas sometime direct affiliate links are harmful.

If you are using WordPress platform, you should rather use their official WordPress plugin which makes it easier to do monetise your blog. With the plugin you can easily insert products with in your blog post, which will increase the CTR and conversions.

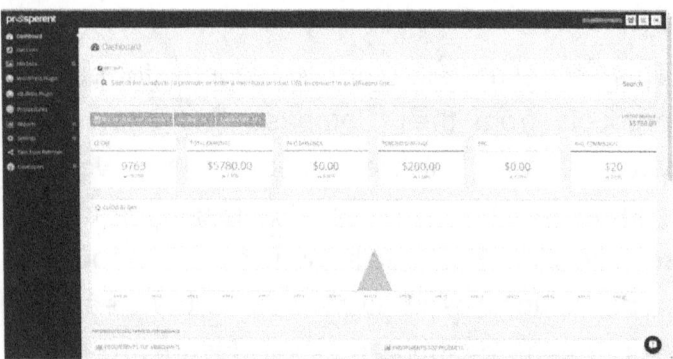

ThemeForest Affiliate Marketing with Example

Becoming an Affiliate

All members can act as affiliates by following the steps outlined in these terms. Just remember that if you want to actively participate in the Affiliate Program there are few things you'll need to keep in mind which are explained below.

Refer new users to any of the Envato Market sites and you'll receive a percentage of their first cash deposit or purchase!

Referral Code: Every member automatically has a referral code which is generated using your username. This referral code is available on the referral page.

Simply paste a link or image button on your site using that code. If a new user clicks your referral link and proceeds to sign up an account and purchase an item or deposit money via any of the Envato Market sites, you will receive a percentage of that person's first cash deposit or purchase.

Referral program percentage: The earnings you will get for successfully participating in the Affiliate Program is set out on the payments page.

How the Affiliate Program Works

Create an Envato Account and send traffic to any page on Envato Market while adding your account username to the end of the URL.

When a new user clicks your referral link, signs up for an account and purchases an item (or deposits money) via any of the Envato Market sites, you will receive 30% of that person's first cash deposit or purchase price. If they deposit $20 into their account, you get $6. If they buy a $200 item, you get $60.

Generate a referral URL

Enter your username and paste any Envato Market site URL below to generate a referral link

Your username *

Envato Market page *

http://themeforest.net/

Referral link

Copy this referral link and paste it anywhere on your website

You can also earn more through our Envato Studio affiliate program. Learn more

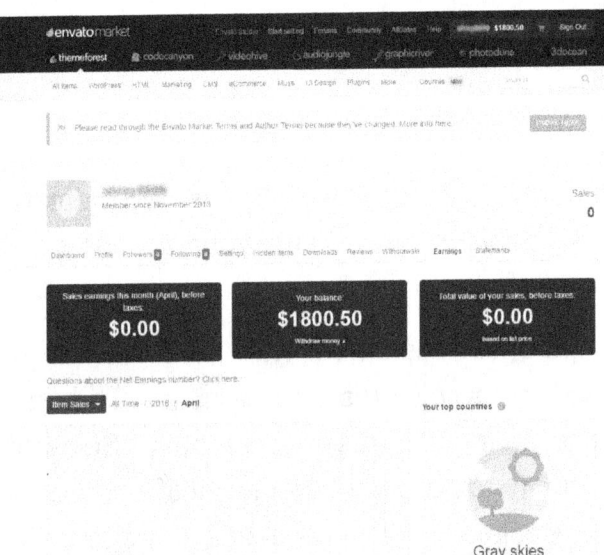

All Items · WordPress · HTML · Marketing · CMS · eCommerce · Muse · UI Design · Plugins · More · Courses

Hi! Please read through the Envato Market Terms and Author Terms because they've changed. More info here.

Member since November 2013

Sales
0

Dashboard · Profile · Followers · Following · Settings · Hidden Items · Downloads · Reviews · Withdrawals · **Earnings** · Statements

Sales earnings this month (April), before taxes:	Your balance:	Total value of your sales, before taxes:
$0.00	**$1800.50**	**$0.00**
	Withdraw money »	based on list price

Questions about the Net Earnings number? Click here.

Item Sales ▾ · All Time / 2016 / **April**

Your top countries

Gray skies
are going to

Five Steps to Internet Marketing Success

High quality content attract friends, followers and fans who are interested in your products and services

Your potential customers want to see what you are selling via pictures and samples. They also want to connect with you personally. Seize the opportunity to build your credibility through Guest Blog Posts, Press Releases, Infographics, Personal Blog Posts and Ebooks.

1. **Guest Blog Post**
   a. Original Content
      i. Original ideas and experience
      ii. New Content improves your Google Search Rankings
   b. Solve a problem, make it relevant
   c. Excellent grammar and spelling
      i. Spelling helps to higher ranking
      ii. Easy to read
   d. Interesting headlines
   e. Well edited article
      i. Clear and consise
   f. Use high quality images

    g. Know the interests of your readers
       i. Share information valuable to your readers
    h. Authoritative website
       i. Add value to the web
       ii. Quality traffic, links and relevance
       iii. Build more trust
    i. Avoid distractions
       i. Too many promotions, advertisements or calls-to-action in the article
    j. Posting YouTube Videos
       i. Support what you're trying to market
       ii. Build your credibility

2. Press Releases
    a. Interesting content and information
       i. Give the who, what, when, where, and why upfront
       ii. Write for members of the media
       iii. Have something truly newsworthy to say
    b. Useful
    c. Be creative
    d. Use high quality images
       i. Photos, videos, graphics
    e. Increase brand reputation

f. Never include a testimonial
g. Share
   i. Give full contact information
   ii. Keep an archive of your company press releases

3. **Infographics**
a. Credible and verified information
   i. Background information
   ii. Trustworthy
   iii. Relevant sources
   iv. Cite your sources
b. Tell a story
c. Unique graphic design
   i. Synthetize
   ii. Conceptualize
d. Branding interaction with clients
   i. Synthetize
   ii. Conceptualize
e. Interesting topic
f. Be creative
g. Distribute, post and share

4. **Personal Posts**
   a. Original content
      i. Share your own experiences
      ii. Personal information and expertise
   b. Solve a problem, Make it relevant and useful
   c. Excellent grammar and spelling
      i. Search engines reward great writing skill
   d. Know the interests of your readers
      i. Share the content
      ii. With interaction and sharing
5. **E-Books**
   a. Define audience
      i. Write to a specific audience, to a specific topic
   b. Original content
      i. Relevant topics
   c. Interesting content
   d. Use high quality images
   e. Editorial design
   f. Useful step-by-step information
   g. Publish your work
      i. Distribute your e-book throughout your social network
      ii. Use email, blogs, your web site and social media channels
      iii. Give value to gain customers respect and attention

16 Tips for Success in Internet Marketing

A great majority of successful people are business owners rather than employees. Some business owners are making their money online. How do they do it? *Justin Gibbs* shared some tips:

1. **Think Differently**: Most people are prepared by school and by parents to become good employees. Gain a business owner's viewpoint from books and experts. As well as reading, you need to implement what you learn.

2. **Take Responsibility**: You are responsible for what you have now in your life, no one else. What do you want? What do you have to do to get it? Commit to it and start making it happen.

3. **Benchmark**: If others with less resources than you can succeed, why can't you? Be prepared to commit long term despite the challenges. Be inspired by other people's successes as examples of possibility.

4. **No Compromise:** Desperate people care more about themselves than their customers, and it is easy to detect. When you're not desperate, you can do things because it's the right thing to do.

5. **Kaizen:** Continually improve, especially in the way WA'I you think. Seek to VI-I I become a perpetual g1 I I learner, always moving forward.

6. **Do Less:** A real business is not about exchanging your time for money. Look for the 4% of effort that delivers 64% of results. Do what you want to do, things where you have a higher impact, and delete, automate or delegate the rest.

7. **Stick to What Works:** Work with the winning strategies and kill the losers. Keep doing the core things that get you the best results.

8. **Give Up:** When something is clearly not working, don't be afraid to call your losses. It's better to realize early when you're wrong and seek a different tactic.

9. **Observe:** You don't have to guess what sells. Just see what people want and need and what they are already paying for. The answers are all around you.

10. **Clarity**: A confused mind makes no choice - Keep things easy for your customers, whether it's the options you offer, your sales process or how you present your solutions.

11. **Own the RaceCourse**: Have a website YOU own where you put all your good content. Make it a self-hosted website, on a fast server, with a domain you control. Do not build your business on an external platform like Facebook, Linkedin or YouTube.

12. **Rich Content**: Post content that answers questions and solves problems. Put it in multiple formats - video, audio, text and images - and do it reasonably often. Let people know via email and social media when you post new stuff.

13. **Results, Not Stuff**: Less products, more value. It's not about how much stuff you can offer your customers, it about getting the best results with the least possible action. This is especially true for subscription services.

14. **Build an E-Mail Database**: Your email list is powerful. Set up the right offer, make sure it has value and send it out at the right time. You can automate triggers, abandonment sequences and feedback requests, but keep your newsletters organic.

15. **Unsubscribe**: From marketing emails. Don't be taken prisoner by your inbox. Be the one sending emails rather than reading them. Also syndicate to where people are, on Facebook, YouTube or Twitter.

16. **Value Reach**: If you want to make a lot of money, create a lot of value and put it in front of as many people as possible.

Marketing Tips for Affiliate Products/Services

1. Identify your Target and Check out Competitors
   a. Which customers are being targeted as part of your marketing activities
   b. Identify your Competitors. Review and analyze their marketing activities
   c. Create a checklist of their best practices
2. Optimize your Website
   a. Use targeted keywords within headlines
   b. Keep your content fresh and unique
   c. Make it easy for yom visitors to find your contact info
3. Off Page Optimization
   a. List your Websites in Popular Directories and post Ads in high traffic Web-sites
   b. Increase your backlinks using the top quality blog websites and forum sites
   c. Create high quality videos that will display your products and services. Market these videos in popular sites like Youtube.com

4. Update Content
   a. Create a Blog section in your website to educate your customers
   b. Share relevant info about your industry in your blog section
5. Social Media Marketing
   a. Build a social network using Social Media sites
   b. Build Relationships using Social Media Interaction
   c. Provide brief description about your Products and Services through Social Media Sites
   d. Spread relevant content through Social Media Sites even though sometimes the content is not created by your team
6. EMail Marketing
   a. Build your Email subscribe list using Landing pages
   b. Interact with Customers using emails as required
   c. Communicate relevant information about your Products and Services through Email Marketing

Tools you Need for Affiliate Marketing

1. Site Audit and Analysis
2. Keyword Analysis Tools
3. Keyword Rank Checker
4. Content Creation
5. Backlink Research Tools
6. Link Management Tools
7. Social Media Management and Analysis
8. Paid Advertising - Reporting and Analysis
9. Email Marketing
10. Affiliate Tools
11. Web/Lead Analytics - Reporting and Marketing

Survey Tools

Conclusion

Affiliate marketing is a key tool for any web site seeking growth. In this performance based marketing, merchants reward affiliates commission for successful referrals.

Affiliate marketing can be used to complement other campaigns, whether they be offline or online. Making sure that there are banners to support these campaigns, the merchant can ensure a wider audience for their other marketing efforts.

Affiliate marketing allows for targeted traffic from niche web sites. While the merchant can focus on a broad spectrum of web sites, affiliate marketing allows for the targeting of niche traffic sources.

Much will depend on the size of your online business, and the sales volume it generate(d)/(s) before the introduction of the affiliate program.

The results of any affiliate marketing campaign are always directly dependent on the amount of time, money and effort the business invests in the development of their affiliate program.

Legal Notice